A Crabtree Branches Book

Catch the Wave

BODYSURFING

Kerri Mazzarella

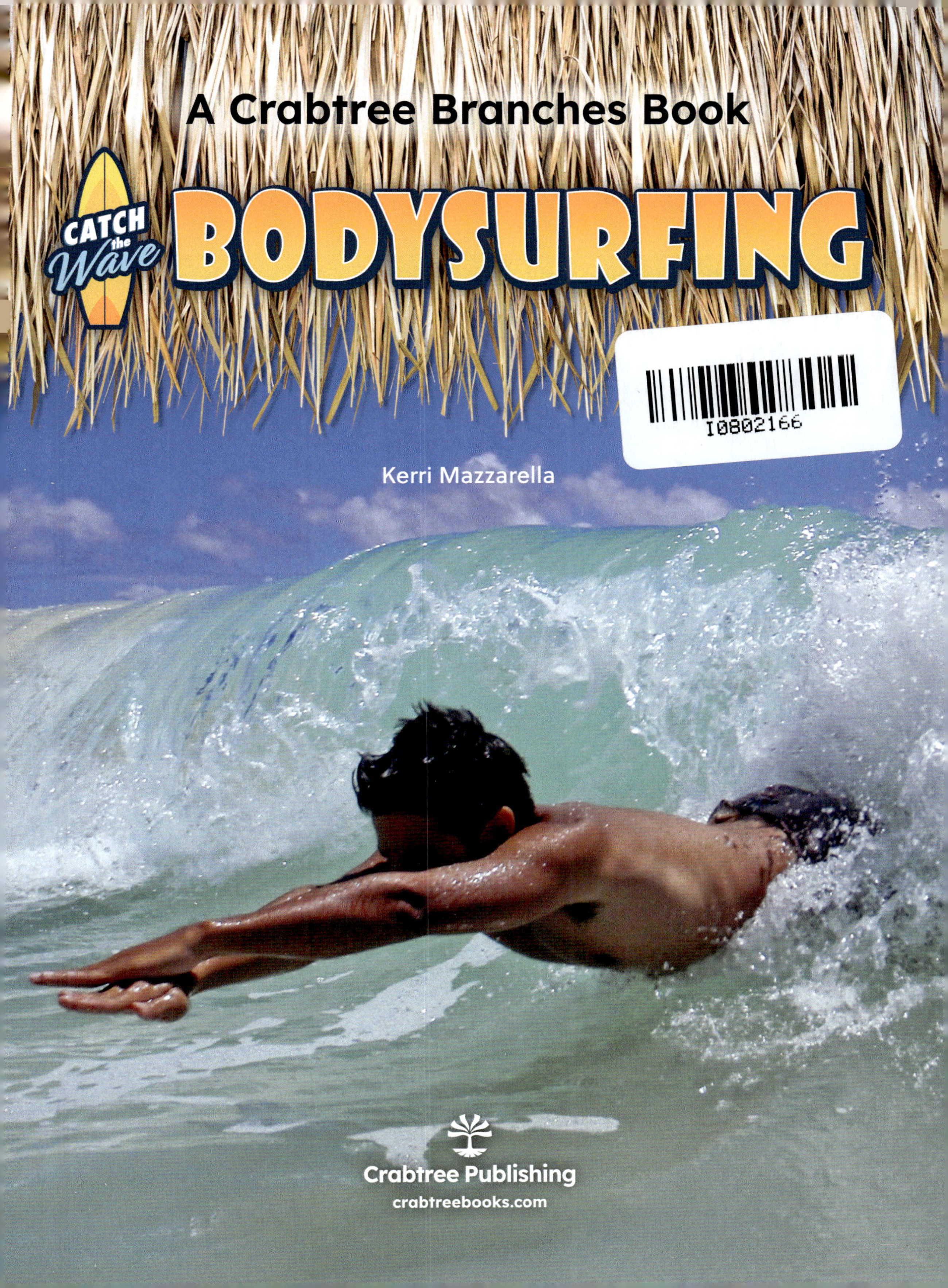

Crabtree Publishing
crabtreebooks.com

School-to-Home Support for Caregivers and Teachers

This high-interest book is designed to motivate striving students with engaging topics while building fluency, vocabulary, and an interest in reading. Here are a few questions and activities to help the reader build upon his or her comprehension skills.

Before Reading:

- *What do I think this book is about?*
- *What do I know about this topic?*
- *What do I want to learn about this topic?*
- *Why am I reading this book?*

During Reading:

- *I wonder why...*
- *I'm curious to know...*
- *How is this like something I already know?*
- *What have I learned so far?*

After Reading:

- *What was the author trying to teach me?*
- *What are some details?*
- *How did the photographs and captions help me understand more?*
- *Read the book again and look for the vocabulary words.*
- *What questions do I still have?*

Extension Activities:

- *What was your favorite part of the book? Write a paragraph on it.*
- *Draw a picture of your favorite thing you learned from the book.*

Table of Contents

WHAT IS BODYSURFING?

Bodysurfing is a sport typically done in the ocean. It is the art of riding a wave with just your body. That's right, no **surfboard**! It is just one of the many different types of surfing you can try.

Bodysurfing is practiced by thousands of people all around the world. It is a great way to get exercise, relieve stress, and have a little fun!

Bodysurfing is the oldest and simplest form of surfing. It was developed by **ancient** Polynesians.

Captain James Cook

Fact

While exploring Tahiti, Polynesia in 1769, Captain James Cook saw villagers gliding with waves in the ocean. Cook became the first European to try bodysurfing.

Bodysurfing first became popular in the United States in the mid-1920s. Many people who visited towns near the **coast** gave it a try.

WHO CAN BODYSURF?

Bodysurfing is a fun beach activity. Anyone who can swim can give bodysurfing a try.

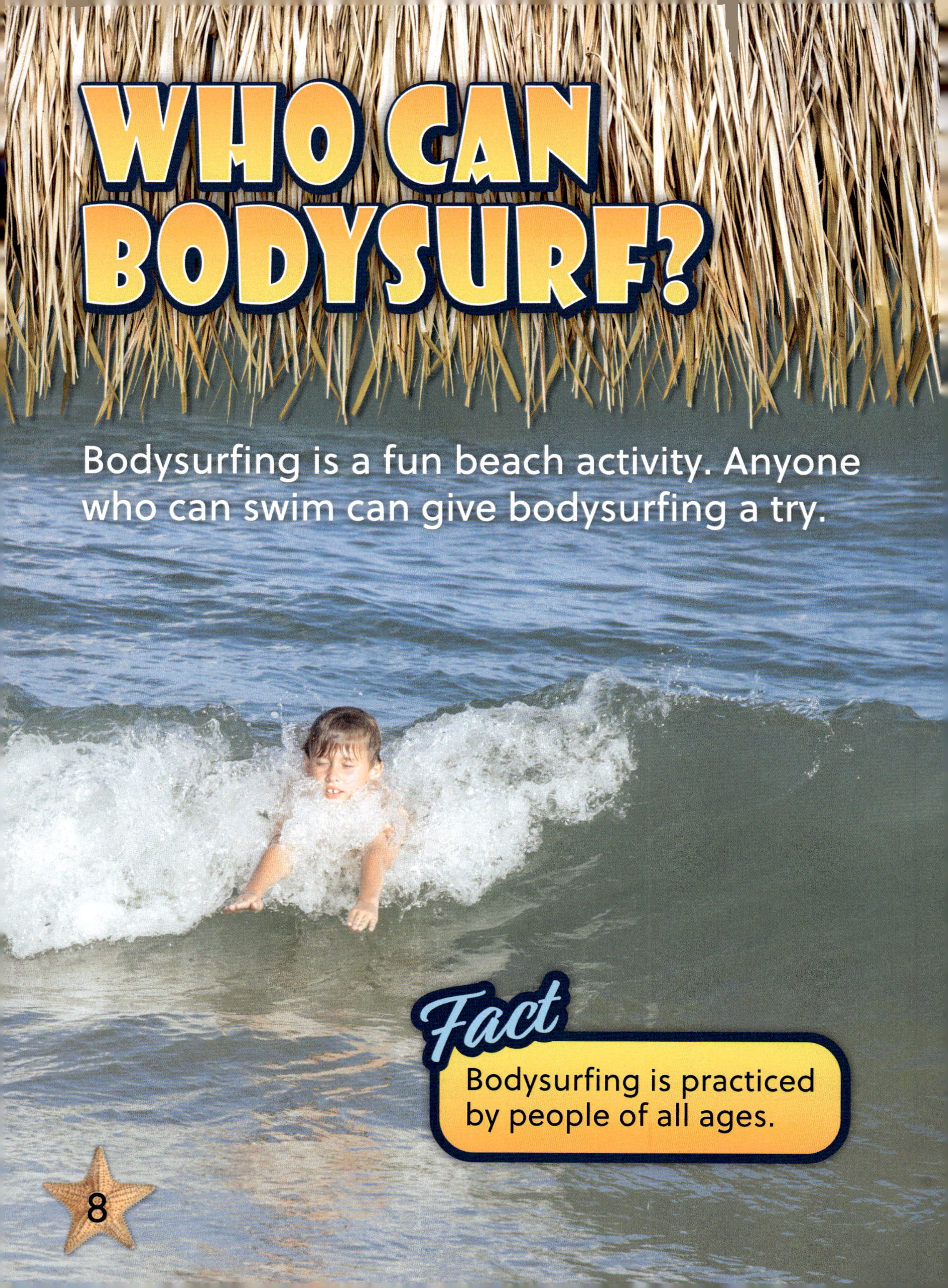

Fact

Bodysurfing is practiced by people of all ages.

Learning to ride waves can be exciting and help you become comfortable in the ocean. However, anyone who goes in the water should know how to deal with ocean waves safely.

bodysurfing dolphin

Fact

Bodysurfing tricks include the reverse spin, bodysurfing dolphin, tube ride, and cutback.

Some bodysurfers take the sport more seriously. They train to ride bigger waves for longer periods of time, and to perform different tricks.

CHOOSING YOUR EQUIPMENT

Choosing the right equipment for bodysurfing is easy. All you need for beginner bodysurfing is your body! It is important to wear a well-fitting bathing suit that will not catch on the waves.

Fact

Some people like to bodysurf in the winter or in places where the water is very cold. They will need to wear a **wetsuit** to keep warm!

Some experienced bodysurfers wear special swim fins to get into waves faster. The fins also help them to **tread water** while waiting for the next wave.

Fact

full wetsuits for kids	$40 - 200
swim fins	$65 - 100
handplanes	$60 - 250

The handplane is another type of equipment that has become popular among bodysurfers. It helps bodysurfers glide faster and have more control while riding a wave.

Fact

Some handplanes are made from recycled material or wood.

WHERE TO BODYSURF

Bodysurfing can be done at almost any beach around the world. Small, steady waves are best for bodysurfing.

Fact

Florida, California, and Hawaii all have great beaches for bodysurfing in the U.S.

Fact

In California, the Black Ball flag is flown to signal, or warn, that surfers with surfboards must leave the water. This is to protect swimmers and bodysurfers from being hit and injured by a surfboard during busy times. Soft surfboards are usually allowed.

Beginner bodysurfers should look for a sandy beach and stay away from **reefs**.

Fact

A break happens when the crest, or highest point, of a wave falls over onto itself.

Bodysurfing is best done on waves that break farther from shore, rather than close to the beach. This gives bodysurfers more time to practice riding the wave.

HOW TO BODYSURF

Learning how to bodysurf can be tricky at first. You can watch videos online for help. You might also take bodysurfing lessons from an experienced bodysurfer in your area.

Fact

The cost of bodysurfing lessons in the U.S. will range from $50 to $100 per hour.

When you get to the beach, take a moment to watch the waves. Notice the crest of each wave and how it moves.

Fact

Taking a deep breath as you begin to ride the wave is important. Filling your lungs with air helps keep you **buoyant** and on top of the wave. Keep your head just above the water.

If the waves look right for bodysurfing, walk into the water until it is chest-high. Choose a wave. As it comes toward you, start to kick with your feet and paddle hard toward shore. When you feel the wave start to lift you, take a deep breath and point one or both arms forward. Keep your body straight and ride the wave for as long as you can!

The excitement of catching your first wave is something you will not forget. With a little practice, you will be riding waves successfully in no time.

FOR YOUR SAFETY

Bodysurfing is fun, but there are a few things you should remember to stay safe. Never bodysurf alone. You should always go with a friend or caregiver. Before diving into the ocean, stretch your muscles to prevent injury.

Fact

UV rays from the Sun can be harmful to your skin. Be sure to use sunscreen to prevent a sunburn.

Did you know that a **rip current** can be deadly?

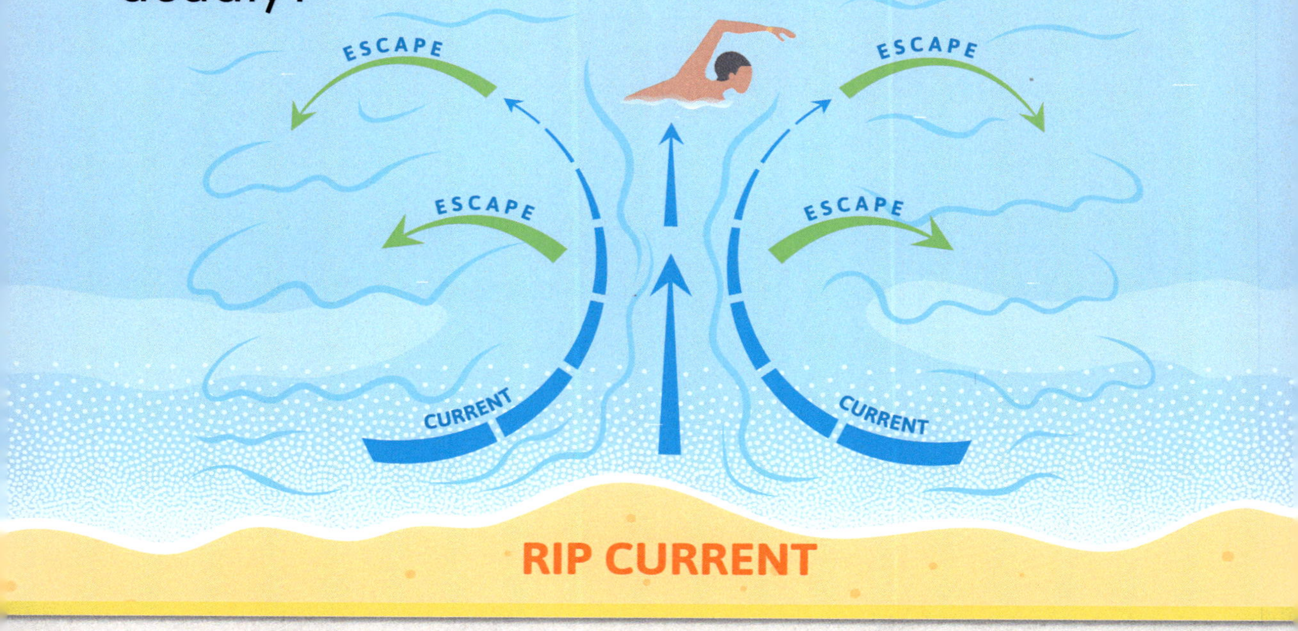

Before entering the water, check the surf report for information about waves and **tides**. Beginner bodysurfers should ride waves no larger than 1 to 4 feet (0.3 to 1.2 m). Bigger waves can hold you under the water longer. Learning how to hold your breath properly is important to stay safe while bodysurfing.

Fact

Surfline is a popular website that surfers use to check the surf report.

It is important to be aware of your surroundings while bodysurfing. Watch out for reefs, rocks, sharks, and other surfers, especially ones with a board!

Colliding with a reef or rock can cause great harm to your body.

It is rare for a surfer to encounter a shark. You can stay safe by learning more about shark behavior. Always leave the water if you see a shark.

Surfboard fins are very sharp and can cause deep cuts that require stitches.

FAMOUS BODYSURFERS

Bodysurfing is not as well-known as other types of surfing. It is not yet recognized as an Olympic sport.

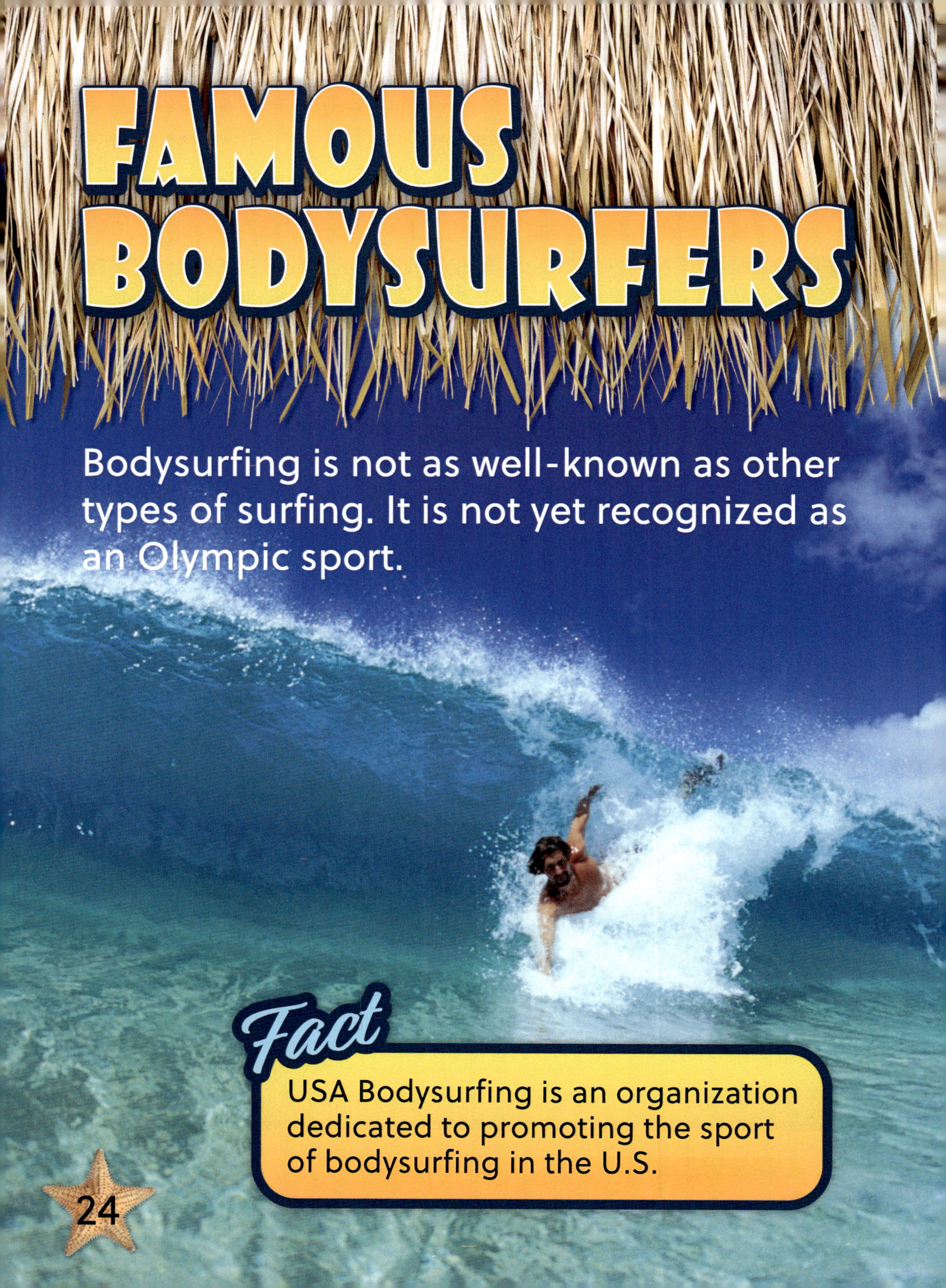

Fact

USA Bodysurfing is an organization dedicated to promoting the sport of bodysurfing in the U.S.

Kalani Lattanzi

Fact

Kalani Lattanzi has made a name for himself by bodysurfing the world's biggest waves at Nazaré, Portugal.

The most famous bodysurfer is Mark Cunningham. He has won many bodysurfing competitions and is known for his swimming skills. Mike Stewart is another well-known bodysurfer. He is a nine-time World Champion in the sport!

Mark Cunningham

RESPECTING OUR OCEANS

Our oceans cover more than 70 percent of Earth's surface. They provide countless benefits to people and all living things.

Fact

The ocean produces more than half the oxygen we breathe.

You can respect the ocean by keeping it clean. Do not leave your trash at the beach. Pick up trash even if it is not yours. Use ocean-safe sunscreen and equipment.

Fact

In 2021, Surfrider Foundation cleaned up 170,000 pounds (77,110 kg) of trash across just the U.S. 84 percent of all items collected were plastic!

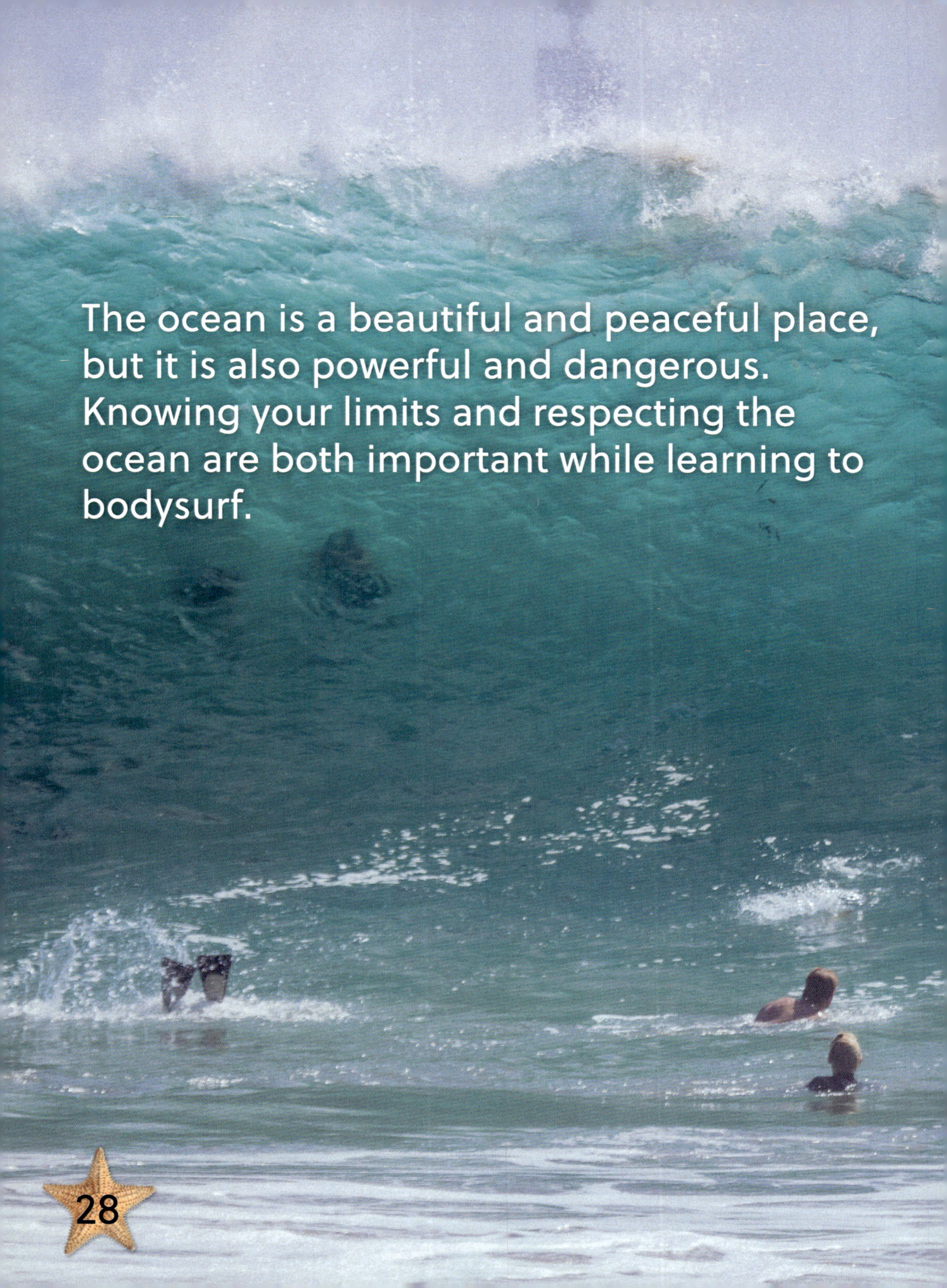

The ocean is a beautiful and peaceful place, but it is also powerful and dangerous. Knowing your limits and respecting the ocean are both important while learning to bodysurf.

Bodysurfing is a fantastic way to enjoy the ocean and the beach. What are you waiting for? Dive in and give it a try!

Glossary

ancient (eyn-shuhnt): Very old; existing a long time ago

buoyant (boi-ent): Able to stay afloat or rise to the surface of water

coast (kohst): Land that lies along the sea or ocean

reef (reef): A strip of rock, sand, or coral close to the surface of the ocean

rip current (rip-kur-uhnt): A strong flow of water running from a beach back to the open ocean

surfboard (surf-bord): A long narrow board with rounded ends on which surfers stand as they ride breaking waves

tide (tide): The constant change in sea level that is caused by the pull of the Sun and the Moon on Earth

tread water (tred-wawtur): To swim in one place with your body in a vertical position

wetsuit (wet-soot): A close-fitting suit, usually made of a type of rubber called neoprene, that is worn in cold water to retain body heat

Index

Websites to Visit

https://kids.kiddle.co/Surfing

https://www.surfertoday.com/surfing/how-to-bodysurf

https://www.wawhandplanes.com/pages/how-to-bodysurf

https://thebodysurfblog.com/bodysurfing-general-history/#aioseo-the-ancient-polynesian-pastime

About the Author

Kerri Mazzarella was raised on the East Coast of southern Florida. Living near the beach has given her the opportunity to watch all types of surfing throughout her life. All four of her children have done their fair share of bodysurfing over the years for fun! Surfing is a great way to connect with the ocean and get some exercise. Her youngest son is a competitive shortboard surfer and travels all over the world to surf!

Written by: Kerri Mazzarella
Designed by: Bobbie Houser
Series Development: James Earley
Proofreader: Janine Deschenes
Educational Consultant: Marie Lemke M.Ed.

Photographs:
t = Top, c = Center, b = Bottom, l = Left, r = Right

Alamy: Cal Cam: p. 4; travelib sri lanka: p. 5; PAINTING: p. 6 tl; Michele and Tom Grimm: p. 6-7; Liz Roll: p. 8; Cavan Images: p. 9-10, 24; Robert Taylor: p. 12-13; Zoonar/ Christopher Bellette: p. 14; Leon Werdinger: p. 19; Chris Jones: p. 20; Duncan Selby: p. 25, 28-29

Shutterstock: tomas del amo: cover, p. 1; s-ts: p. 11; Michael Barajas: p. 15; 23pictures: p. 16; AYO Production: p. 17; Dr. Ingmar Koehler: p. 18; Wirestock Creators: p. 21; Good_Stock: p. 22; wanchai: p. 23 tl; Dogora Sun: p. 23 bl; LuckyStep: p. 23 r; Willyam Bradberry: p. 26; Prostock-studio: p. 27

Crabtree Publishing

crabtreebooks.com 800-387-7650

Printed in the U.S.A./052025/CP20250422

Published in Canada
Crabtree Publishing
616 Welland Ave.
St. Catharines, Ontario
L2M 5V6

Published in the United States
Crabtree Publishing
347 Fifth Ave
Suite 1402-145
New York, NY 10016

Library and Archives Canada Cataloguing in Publication
Available at Library and Archives Canada

Library of Congress Cataloging-in-Publication Data
Available at the Library of Congress

Hardcover: 978-1-0398-8024-5
Paperback: 978-1-0398-8384-0
Ebook (pdf): 978-1-0398-8144-0
Epub: 978-1-0398-8264-5